The Problem Isn't You

The Effects of Narcissism and Emotional Abuse and How to Heal

Evan Huffman

Table of Contents

INTRODUCTION

"The Problem Isn't You: The Effects of Narcissism and Emotional Abuse and How to Heal" is a thorough handbook that aims to help people understand, negotiate, and heal from the devastating effects of narcissistic abuse and emotional manipulation. This book is both a beacon of hope and a practical guide for people who have suffered at the hands of narcissists, offering insight, validation, and meaningful steps toward recovery.

An overview of the book's purpose

Understanding Narcissism and Emotional Abuse: At its foundation, this book aims to clarify the complicated and sometimes misunderstood ideas of narcissism and emotional abuse. In clinical terms, narcissism refers to Narcissistic Personality Disorder (NPD), which is characterized by a pervasive pattern of grandiosity, a desire for admiration, and a lack of empathy. Individuals without a recognized diagnosis may display narcissistic tendencies, causing substantial emotional and psychological harm to others around them.

Emotional abuse, on the other hand, refers to a variety of acts designed to control, humiliate, and manipulate another person. This sort of abuse is frequently subtle and insidious, leaving lasting wounds that are invisible to the human sight but deeply felt by the victim.

By delving into these actions and their consequences, "The Problem Isn't You" attempts to provide readers with the knowledge they need to detect and comprehend abusive relationships. This knowledge is critical because it provides the framework for victims to begin rebuilding their lives, free of the uncertainty and self-doubt that their abusers frequently impose.

Validating the victim's experience: One of the most destructive effects of narcissistic and emotional abuse is that it distorts the victim's perspective of reality, causing them to question their own sanity and self-worth. Narcissists excel at gaslighting, a manipulative technique that makes the victim to question their own memory, perception, and judgment. Over time, this can destroy the victim's confidence and sense of self, leaving them increasingly reliant on the abuser for validation and reality checks.

"The Problem Isn't You" seeks to combat this manipulation by validating the victim's experiences. The book reassures readers that their experiences and emotions are genuine by providing extensive explanations of frequent narcissistic actions and their consequences, as well as personal tales and case studies. This confirmation is an important initial step in the healing process, allowing victims to regain their sense of reality and begin rebuilding their self-esteem.

Offering practical strategies for coping and healing: Understanding and affirmation are crucial, but they are simply the start of the healing process. "The Problem Isn't You" goes much farther, providing practical solutions for dealing with and healing from narcissistic and emotional abuse. These tactics are derived from a wide range of therapeutic approaches, including cognitive-behavioral therapy (CBT), dialectical behavior therapy (DBT), and mindfulness practices, among others.

The book walks readers through the process of implementing these tactics in their daily lives, helping them establish healthy coping mechanisms, create and keep boundaries, and build a support network. It also highlights the value of self-care and self-compassion, encouraging readers to prioritize their own health and be kind with themselves as they go through the recovery process.

Encouraging empowerment and growth: Ultimately, "The Problem Isn't You" is about empowerment and development. Its goal is to assist readers not only heal from the symptoms of abuse, but also to become stronger and more resilient. The book urges readers to see their experiences as a catalyst for personal growth, enabling them to get a better understanding of themselves and their needs, as well as to form healthier and more rewarding relationships in the future.

"The Problem Isn't You" offers a thorough path to recovery and empowerment by combining information, affirmation, practical counsel, and support. It demonstrates the human spirit's tenacity and perseverance, as well as a reminder that healing is always possible, no matter how deep the scars.

CHAPTER ONE: UNDERSTANDING NARCISSISM

Definition and Characteristics of Narcissism:

The term narcissism comes from the Greek tale of Narcissus, a young man who fell in love with his own reflection in a pool of water. Narcissism is a complicated personality characteristic or disease defined by an exaggerated feeling of self-importance, a strong desire for excessive attention and praise, difficult relationships, and a lack of empathy for others. While some narcissism is beneficial and even required for self-esteem and confidence, pathological narcissism may cause substantial emotional and psychological harm to people around the narcissist.

Definition of Narcissistic Personality Disorder (NPD)

Narcissistic Personality Disorder (NPD) is a mental illness in which people have an exaggerated feeling of their own importance, a strong desire for excessive attention and praise, strained relationships, and a lack of empathy for others. However, underneath this façade of excessive confidence comes a frail self-esteem that is sensitive to even the smallest criticism. The Diagnostic and Statistical Manual of Mental Disorders, Fifth Edition (DSM-5) specifies the criteria for diagnosing NPD. According to the DSM-5, an individual must demonstrate at least five of the following features in order to be diagnosed with NPD:

1. Grandiose feeling of self-importance: exaggerates accomplishments and skills, expecting to be acknowledged as superior while lacking comparable achievements.

2. Obsession with dreams of limitless success, power, brilliance, beauty, or perfect love.

3. Belief that they are exceptional and unique and must be understood or associated with other remarkable or high-status persons or institutions.

4. Requirement for overwhelming adoration.

5. Sense of entitlement: Unreasonable expectations of particularly favorable treatment or automatic adherence to their expectations.

6. Interpersonal exploitative behavior: Taking advantage of others to attain one's own goals.

7. Lack of empathy: Unwillingness to acknowledge or empathize with the emotions and needs of others.

8. Envy toward others or the feeling that others are envious of them.

9. arrogant, haughty action or attitude.

Features of Narcissism

Narcissistic conduct can range from modestly self-centered to highly damaging personality characteristics. The key traits of narcissism are:

- Grandiosity: Narcissists frequently overstate their own significance. They feel they are superior to others and can only be understood by like unique individuals. They may continuously boast about their own achievements, expecting others to adore them.

- Need for Admiration: Narcissists are always seeking admiration and approval from others. They are frequently concerned about how they are seen and will go to considerable measures to ensure that they are viewed favorably.

- Lack of Empathy: One of the defining characteristics of narcissism is a lack of empathy. Narcissists frequently fail to notice or care about the emotions and needs of others. They may come out as cold, disconnected, or uncaring to the plight of others.

- Entitlement: Narcissists frequently believe they deserve special treatment and advantages. They may feel enraged or irritated if they do not receive the recognition or treatment they believe they are entitled to.

- Manipulative and exploitative behavior: Narcissists usually utilize people to attain their own goals. They may manipulate or use relationships to achieve their goals, frequently with little concern for the consequences to others.

- Arrogance: Narcissists frequently exhibit arrogant, haughty conduct or attitudes. They may disparage or degrade others in order to retain their sense of superiority.

Healthy versus Pathological Narcissism

While the term "narcissism" has negative connotations, it is critical to distinguish between healthy and pathological narcissism. Healthy narcissism is a normal component of human growth and can help to boost self-esteem and confidence. Pathological narcissism, or NPD, is a maladaptive behavior that harms both the individual and those around them.

Healthy Narcissism

Healthy narcissism is characterized by a balanced sense of self-esteem and value. Individuals with healthy narcissism are secure in their talents and respect themselves, but they lack an exaggerated feeling of superiority. Healthy narcissism consists of the following characteristics:

- Self-Esteem: People with healthy narcissism have a realistic perception of their own value. They recognize their own skills and flaws and feel good about themselves without seeking continual approval from others.

- Confidence: Healthy narcissism includes a sense of self-assurance that helps people to pursue their goals and assert themselves correctly in a variety of contexts.

- Empathy: Healthy narcissists may comprehend and sympathize with the emotions and viewpoints of others. They appreciate their relationships and attempt to keep them positive.

- Resilience: Healthy narcissism promotes emotional resilience. Individuals can cope with criticism and disappointments without significantly lowering their self-esteem.

- Boundaries: Healthy narcissists respect their own and others' boundaries. They may establish themselves without being exploitative or manipulative.

Pathological Narcissism

Pathological narcissism, or NPD, is defined by severe self-centeredness and an overwhelming desire for praise and affirmation. It frequently results in unhealthy relationships and substantial emotional and psychological trauma for others around the narcissist. Pathological narcissism includes the following characteristics:

- Grandiosity: Pathological narcissists have an excessive feeling of self-importance and believe they are better than others. This grandiosity frequently conceals deep-seated fears.

- Excessive Need for Admiration: Pathological narcissists are always seeking admiration and approval from others. When they do not receive the attention they seek, they may feel agitated or furious.

- Lack of Empathy: Pathological narcissists are unable to identify or care about the emotions and needs of others. They may exploit people for personal benefit without contemplating the consequences of their conduct.

- Manipulative and exploitative behavior: Pathological narcissists frequently manipulate and exploit people to attain their own goals. They could use charm or trickery to acquire what they desire.

- Entitlement: Pathological narcissists feel they deserve special treatment and benefits. They may become resentful or hostile if they do not receive the recognition or treatment they feel they are entitled to.

- Fragile Self-Esteem: Despite their apparent confidence, pathological narcissists frequently have low self-esteem. They are extremely sensitive to criticism and may respond angrily or defensively to perceived slights.

The Effects of Narcissism on Relationships

Narcissism, particularly pathological narcissism, has a significant influence on relationships. People with NPD frequently struggle to establish healthy, balanced relationships because of their manipulative and self-centered tendencies. Common concerns in partnerships with narcissists are:

- Lack of Emotional Intimacy: Narcissists frequently fail to create meaningful emotional connections with others. Their lack of empathy and focus on their own wants might make it difficult for them to form true, deep connections.

- Narcissists typically manipulate and dominate their relationships in order to maintain a sense of superiority and meet their own wants. This might cause a poisonous and imbalanced dynamic in the relationship.

- Narcissists frequently go through cycles of idealizing and depreciating their spouses. During the idealization phase, they may show their spouse attention and devotion. However, this is frequently followed by a devaluation period in which they become critical, aloof, and dismissive.

- Gaslighting and Emotional Abuse: Narcissists frequently employ gaslighting, a type of psychological manipulation that causes the victim to question their own perspective and reality. This can cause substantial emotional and psychological distress.

- Narcissists frequently exhibit insecurity and jealousy, which leads to dominating and possessive tendencies. They may get angry or resentful if they believe their partner is gaining attention or appreciation from others.

- Conflict and aggressiveness: Narcissists frequently cause conflict and aggressiveness in their relationships. Narcissists may respond violently or aggressively to perceived slights or critiques, making it difficult to handle problems in a healthy and constructive manner.

Recognize Narcissistic Behaviors

Recognizing narcissistic tendencies is critical for safeguarding oneself against emotional and psychological harm. Some frequent indications of narcissism are:

- Self-centeredness: Narcissists frequently dominate talks and shift the attention to themselves. They may exhibit little interest in other people's experiences or emotions.

- Narcissists usually overstate their achievements and skills. They may fabricate or embellish stories to make themselves look more remarkable.

- continual Need for Praise: Narcissists want continual adoration and approval from others. They may become agitated or furious if they do not get the attention they seek.

- Lack of Empathy: Narcissists frequently fail to comprehend or care about the feelings and needs of others. They might come out as cold, apathetic, or uncaring.

- Entitlement: Narcissists feel they deserve special attention and benefits. They may feel resentful or furious if they do not receive the recognition and treatment to which they believe they are due.

- Manipulative Behavior: Narcissists usually employ manipulation to achieve their goals. They may charm, mislead, or exploit people for personal benefit.

- Arrogance: Narcissists frequently exhibit arrogant, haughty conduct or attitudes. They may disparage or humiliate others in order to retain their sense of superiority.

Coping With Narcissism

Coping with narcissism, whether in oneself or in others, necessitates a mix of self-awareness, limits, and support. Here are some approaches to coping with narcissism:

- Set clear limits to protect yourself against manipulation and exploitation. Maintain strict and consistent boundaries.

- Seek Support: Surround yourself with friends and family who can offer affirmation and encouragement. Consider getting professional assistance, such as therapy, to manage the difficulties of working with a narcissist.

- Self-Care: Put your own well-being first and engage in activities that encourage self-care and compassion. Take the time to improve your physical, emotional, and mental wellness.

- Educate yourself. Learn more about narcissism and its consequences to better understand and manage your encounters with narcissists. Knowledge is a great weapon for self-defense and educated decision-making.

- Maintain realistic expectations. Recognize that narcissists are unlikely to modify their conduct without major self-awareness and expert assistance. Maintain a realistic outlook and concentrate on what you can manage.

- Consider Professional Help: Therapy may be a useful tool for people living with narcissism. A therapist can offer advice, support, and coping skills for dealing with narcissistic tendencies.

CHAPTER 2: NARCISSISTIC PARENT: IDENTIFYING SIGNS.

Narcissistic parents engage in a variety of activities that indicate their intense desire for attention, affirmation, and control. These indications can help you determine whether your parent is a narcissist, helping you to better understand their influence on your life and take measures toward recovery.

Grandiosity and superiority

Narcissistic parents frequently demonstrate an excessive feeling of self-importance. They feel they are superior to others and expect to be acknowledged as such, despite the fact that they have no significant accomplishments to back up their claims. They may continually boast about their own accomplishments and seek attention and respect from their family members.

- Constant Need for Praise: They want praise and frequently seek compliments. Any criticism, no matter how helpful, is likely to provoke defensiveness or fury.

- Inflated Achievements: They overestimate their achievements and skills, convinced that they are unique or exceptional and can only be comprehended by other remarkable individuals.

Lack of empathy

Inability to empathize with others is a defining feature of narcissism. Narcissistic parents are generally unaware of their children's emotional needs and experiences.

- Emotional Insensitivity: They may ignore or minimize your emotions, demonstrating little to no concern for how their actions affect you.

- Inconsistent Support: They may be supportive when it benefits them or their image, but absent or critical when you require true assistance or empathy.

- Control and manipulation.

- Narcissistic parents frequently use deceptive strategies to keep control over their children. These actions might be subtle or overt, but their fundamental purpose is to prioritize their own wants above everyone else.

- Gaslighting is when someone manipulates you into doubting your own memory, perspective, or sanity. They may deny earlier incidents or accuse you of being excessively sensitive or unreasonable.

- Triangulation: They may set family members against one another in an attempt to keep control and feel superior. This causes confusion and dissension among the family.

- Guilt-Tripping: Narcissistic parents frequently use guilt to manipulate their children by making them feel responsible for the parent's pleasure or well-being.

Entitlement and Exploitation

Narcissistic parents frequently feel entitled to preferential treatment and expect their children to meet their wants and desires without reciprocation.

- Unreasonable Expectations: They may expect excessive attention, obedience, or adoration from their children. Failure to achieve these expectations is frequently met with wrath or punishment.

- Exploitation: They utilize their children to further their own interests, whether that be to improve their image, attain social standing, or meet their own emotional needs.

Lack of Boundaries

Narcissistic parents frequently violate personal boundaries, viewing their children as extensions of themselves rather than self-sufficient people.

- Invasion of Privacy: They may invade on your personal space, read your private messages, or interfere with your relationships without respect for your rights.

- Overcontrol: They make choices for you, frequently excessively interfering in your personal issues long into maturity.

Common Behaviors and their Effects on Family Dynamics

Understanding the typical actions of narcissistic parents and how they affect family dynamics is critical for detecting the long-term repercussions on your mental well-being and relationships.

Favoritism and scapegoating.

Favoritism is common among narcissistic parents, with one child being the "golden child" who can do no wrong and the other being the "scapegoat" who is blamed for everything that goes wrong.

- Golden kid: Although the golden kid is frequently romanticized and lauded, this preference is accompanied with high expectations and conditional affection. They may feel great pressure to live up to their parents' excessive expectations.

- Scapegoat: The scapegoat is held responsible for the family's difficulties and faults. They frequently face harsh criticism and may develop sentiments of worthlessness and self-doubt.

Sibling rivalry, bitterness, and long-term emotional scars are all consequences of the family dynamics. The golden kid may struggle with perfectionism and fear of failure, whereas the scapegoat may have poor self-esteem and continuous self-blame.

Conditional Love and Approval

Narcissistic parents frequently bestow affection and praise based on the child's performance or conduct.

- Performance-Based Love: They may only express affection when you do something that makes them proud or improves their image.

- Withdrawal of Affection: If you fail to match their expectations or dispute their authority, they may remove their affection and attention as punishment.

This conditional love instills uneasiness and anxiety in youngsters, resulting in a persistent desire for affirmation and fear of abandonment.

Emotional Neglect and Invalidating Feelings.

Narcissistic parents usually ignore their children's emotional needs while invalidating their sentiments.

- Emotional Neglect: They may be physically present but emotionally inaccessible, denying children the emotional support and care they require.

- Invalidation: They disregard or denigrate your emotions, claiming that you are overreacting or overly sensitive.

This can lead to trouble believing your own emotions, low self-esteem, and issues with emotional management.

Enmeshment and lack of autonomy

Narcissistic parents frequently foster an interwoven family dynamic in which personal boundaries are blurred and uniqueness is suppressed.

- Lack of Independence: They may discourage or sabotage your efforts to gain independence, making you feel guilty for trying to separate or establish your own personality.

- Overinvolvement: They get too involved in your life decisions, frequently influencing your profession, relationships, and other personal choices.

This lack of autonomy might impair your capacity to have a strong sense of self and make autonomous decisions, resulting in reliance and low self-esteem.

Criticism and perfectionism

Narcissistic parents frequently use harsh criticism and demand perfection from their children.

- Harsh Criticism: They emphasize your shortcomings and mistakes, frequently humiliating you in front of others to demonstrate their superiority.

- Unrealistic Standards: They establish unrealistic goals, expecting perfection in academics, beauty, conduct, and other aspects of life.

This habit promotes a fear of failure and a pervasive belief that one is never "good enough," which can lead to chronic anxiety, melancholy, and perfectionistic inclinations.

Impact on Family Dynamics

The existence of a narcissistic parent may have a significant influence on family relations, frequently generating a poisonous atmosphere characterized by conflict, manipulation, and emotional instability. Some frequent implications are:

- Divisiveness and Conflict: Narcissistic parents can cause divides among family members, cultivating an atmosphere of distrust and competitiveness.

- Lack of Emotional Safety: The family environment is usually unstable and emotionally unsafe, with members feeling they must walk on eggshells to avoid provoking the narcissist's fury.

- Emotional and psychological damage: Children of narcissistic parents frequently have low self-esteem, anxiety, sadness, and difficulties building healthy relationships.

- Parentification: Children may be driven to assume adult roles, such as emotional caregivers for the narcissistic parent, depriving them of a normal childhood.

Healing From A Narcissistic Parent

Recognizing the symptoms and consequences of having a narcissistic parent is the first step toward recovery. Here are some ways for recovery:

Establish Boundaries

- Establishing and maintaining appropriate boundaries is critical when dealing with a narcissistic parent. This involves:

- Define Limits: Clearly identify prohibited actions and communicate them strongly and consistently.

- Enforcing boundaries: Be prepared to enforce your boundaries with consequences if they are broken, even if it involves restricting contact or separating yourself from the narcissistic parent.

Seek professional help.

Therapy may be quite helpful in processing the pain of having a narcissistic parent. A trained therapist can assist you:

- Validate Your Experiences: Recognize and validate the emotional abuse you have received.

- Develop coping strategies: Learn healthy coping strategies for dealing with continuing contacts with the narcissistic parent.

- Build Self-Esteem: Focus on repairing your self-esteem and creating a strong sense of self that is independent of your parents' influence.

- Focus on Self-Care

- Prioritize your well-being by participating in activities that enhance physical, emotional, and mental health.

- Physical Self-Care: Exercise frequently, consume a balanced diet, and get enough sleep.

- Emotional Self-Care: Engage in things that offer you joy and relaxation, such as hobbies, spending time with loved ones, or practicing meditation.

- Mental Self-Care: Make time for intellectual stimulation and personal improvement, whether by reading, developing new skills, or pursuing educational objectives.

Create a Support Network.

Surround yourself with helpful, sympathetic people who can offer affirmation and encouragement. This may include:

- Friends and family: Seek out ties with people who understand your circumstances and can provide true assistance.
- Support Groups: Join support groups for adult children of narcissists to share your experiences and learn from others who have had similar issues.

Reclaim your identity.

Focus on creating a strong sense of self that is independent of your narcissistic parent's influence.

- Explore Your Interests: Engage in hobbies and activities that really interest you, which can help you find your true interests and abilities.

- Set personal goals. Define and pursue your own objectives and dreams, regardless of your parents' expectations or wants.

- Cultivate self-compassion. Practice self-compassion by being kind and sympathetic to yourself, especially if you're suffering with the emotional consequences of your childhood.

Practice Assertiveness.

Assertiveness is essential when dealing with a narcissistic parent because it helps you to express your demands and limits while preserving respect and dignity. Here's how to develop assertiveness.

- Communicate Clearly: Explain your views, feelings, and boundaries in a calm and polite manner. Use "I" phrases to take control of your emotions and avoid blaming or accusing language.

- Stand Your Ground: Do not be misled by manipulation or guilt trips. Maintain your boundaries and decisions, even if the narcissistic parent attempts to undermine or ignore them.

- Set Limits: If your narcissistic parent refuses to accept your boundaries, be prepared to restrict your relationships with them. This might involve limiting interaction, defining specified themes that are off-limits for conversation, or imposing punishments for disrespectful behavior.

- Practice Self-Validation: Trust your own judgment and intuition, even if the narcissistic parent attempts to downplay or invalidate your experiences. Seek confirmation from inside rather than relying on other sources.

- Seek Support: When you're dealing with a difficult circumstance with your narcissistic parent, surround yourself with friends who can support and validate you. This might include friends, family members, or support organizations for adult children of narcissists.

- Self-Care: Put your own well-being first by participating in activities that improve physical, emotional, and mental health. Take pauses when required, use relaxation techniques, and seek professional assistance if necessary.

Remember that you can't influence or control the narcissistic parent's conduct. Focus on what you can control—your own behaviors, ideas, and responses—and stop attempting to alter the narcissist.

CHAPTER THREE: THE ORIGINS OF NARCISSISM

How Narcissists Develop: Genetic, Psychological, and Social Factors

Narcissism is a complex personality trait that can be impacted by a variety of genetic, psychological, and social variables. Understanding the causes of narcissism can give significant insights into how it develops and emerges in individuals.

Genetic factors

- While no one "narcissism gene" has been found, research indicates that genetics may play a role in predisposing people to narcissistic tendencies.

- Heritability: Research indicates that narcissistic personality characteristics are moderately to highly heritable, implying that genetic factors play a role in their development.

- Personality qualities: Some personality qualities, such as extraversion and neuroticism, have been related to narcissism and may be inherited.

- Neurobiological Factors: Some studies show that anomalies in brain structure and function, like as changes in the prefrontal cortex and amygdala, may be linked to narcissistic tendencies.

While genetics may predispose people to narcissistic tendencies, environmental variables also have a substantial impact on narcissistic personality development.

Psychological Factors

Psychological variables, like as early childhood experiences and attachment patterns, can have a substantial impact on narcissistic development.

- Parenting Styles: Overvaluation or excessive criticism can lead to the development of narcissistic tendencies in children.

- Attachment Theory: Narcissism has been linked to insecure attachment behaviors such as ambivalence or avoidance. Children who receive inconsistent or inattentive care may develop maladaptive coping mechanisms, such as seeking external affirmation or forming a grandiose self-image.

- Identity Formation: Narcissism can develop as a coping technique to conceal underlying emotions of insecurity or inadequacy. Individuals who have experienced trauma or rejection in infancy may develop narcissistic defenses to safeguard their damaged self-esteem.

Cultural values and conventions can influence narcissistic personality development. Individuals who are raised in societies that value individualism, prestige, and monetary success may develop narcissistic tendencies.

Social factors

Peer connections, media influences, and cultural norms all play important roles in the formation of a narcissistic personality.

- Peer connections between children and adolescents can impact the development of narcissistic tendencies. Social rejection or exclusion can cause feelings of inadequacy and a strong desire for reinforcement and praise.

- Media Influences: The spread of social media and celebrity culture has been connected to an increase in narcissism, particularly among young people. The relentless search of approval and attention on social media platforms might exacerbate individuals' narcissistic tendencies.

- Cultural values that emphasize individual effort, competitiveness, and success may lead to the emergence of narcissistic tendencies. Individuals in societies that prioritize material prosperity and prestige may develop a feeling of entitlement and grandiosity.

The Importance of Early Childhood Experiences

Early childhood events, particularly those in the familial setting, have a significant impact on narcissistic personality development.

- Parenting techniques: Authoritarian or permissive parenting techniques that emphasize overvaluation or excessive criticism might lead to the development of narcissistic characteristics in children.

- Parent-Child interactions: The quality of the parent-child connection, especially during the formative years, can have an impact on the child's self-esteem, sense of identity, and social interactions.

- Attachment Patterns: According to attachment theory, early attachment experiences with caregivers can influence a person's relationship patterns and self-concept. Insecure attachment patterns, like ambivalent or avoidant attachment, have been linked to narcissistic personality characteristics.

- Childhood trauma, neglect, or abuse can have long-term consequences on personality development, including maladaptive coping mechanisms like narcissism. Individuals who have experienced rejection, abandonment, or emotional invalidation in their childhood may develop narcissistic defenses to shield themselves from future suffering.

- Sibling dynamics can also have an impact on the development of narcissistic personality traits. Sibling rivalry, favoritism, or scapegoating in the family dynamic can all lead to emotions of insecurity, competitiveness, and a craving for affirmation and attention.

Narcissism is a complex personality characteristic impacted by a variety of genetic, psychological, and social variables. While genetics may predispose individuals to narcissistic tendencies, contextual factors such as early childhood experiences, parenting techniques, attachment patterns, and cultural influences all have a substantial impact on narcissistic personality development.

Understanding the roots of narcissism sheds light on how it develops and emerges in individuals. Recognizing the interaction between genetic predispositions and environmental variables allows us to obtain a better knowledge of narcissistic personality development and its consequences for mental health and well-being.

CHAPTER FOUR: THE DAMAGE DONE

Detailed Investigation of How Narcissistic Abuse Affects Victims

Narcissistic abuse is a widespread and subtle kind of psychological manipulation that can have serious and long-term consequences for its victims. In this chapter, we will look in depth at how narcissistic abuse affects people emotionally, mentally, and occasionally physically.

Emotional consequences

- Low Self-Esteem: Victims of narcissistic abuse may feel inadequate and unworthy. Constant criticism, gaslighting, and manipulation destroy their self-esteem, making them feel helpless and unworthy of love or respect.

- Anxiety and despair: Narcissistic abuse causes ongoing tension and mental instability, which can lead to anxiety disorders and despair. Victims may have anxiety attacks, sleeplessness, and feelings of hopelessness and despair.

- Guilt and Shame: Narcissistic abusers frequently utilize blame-shifting and guilt-tripping to manipulate their victims. As a result, victims may develop emotions of guilt and humiliation, believing that they are to blame for the abuser's actions or that they deserve the mistreatment.

- Isolation and Loneliness: Narcissistic abusers frequently isolate their victims from friends, family, and support networks, making them feel alone and helpless. This isolation can worsen victims' sense of worthlessness and make it harder for them to seek treatment or leave the abusive environment.

- Emotional Dysregulation: Victims of narcissistic abuse may struggle to control their emotions, resulting in extreme mood swings and outbursts. Constant gaslighting and manipulation might make them feel confused and distant from their own emotions and experiences.

Psychological consequences

- Cognitive Distortions: Narcissistic abuse can result in skewed thinking patterns such black-and-white thinking, catastrophizing, and self-blame. Victims may absorb the abuser's negative words, creating a skewed view of themselves and the world around them.

- Trauma Bonding: Victims of narcissistic abuse frequently form a deep relationship to their abuser, which is known as trauma bonding. This connection is characterized by a cycle of abuse and sporadic reinforcement, which leaves victims feeling stuck and unable to leave the abusive relationship.

- Complex PTSD: Narcissistic abuse can result in complex post-traumatic stress disorder (C-PTSD), which is marked by flashbacks, hypervigilance, and emotional numbness. Victims may have long-term psychological repercussions even after they have left the abusive circumstances.

- Identity Erosion: Narcissistic abuse weakens victims' sense of self and identity. Constant criticism and invalidation might leave them feeling unsure of who they are and what they want out of life. Victims may find it difficult to articulate their own demands and limits, instead putting the abuser's wants first.

- Victims of narcissistic abuse may develop problematic interpersonal habits as a result of their ordeal. They may struggle to trust people, create appropriate boundaries, or form stable attachments, which can make it difficult to form and sustain healthy relationships later in life.

Physical Consequences

- Psychosomatic Symptoms: The stress and anxiety caused by narcissistic abuse can show as physical symptoms including migraines, digestive difficulties, and chronic pain. Victims may feel a variety of psychosomatic symptoms that have no obvious medical origin but are related to their emotional discomfort.

- Victims of narcissistic abuse may have sleep difficulties such as sleeplessness or nightmares. Continuous stress and emotional upheaval might make it difficult for them to relax and fall asleep, resulting in chronic sleep deprivation and exhaustion.

- Autoimmune illnesses: According to some study, continuous stress and trauma, such as those experienced during narcissistic abuse, may lead to the development of autoimmune illnesses. Victims of chronic stress may develop increased inflammation and immunological dysfunction.

- Victims of narcissistic abuse may use drugs or alcohol to cope with their emotional agony. Substance misuse can compound the physical and psychological effects of abuse, resulting in further health issues and dysfunction.

- Self-Harm: In severe circumstances, victims of narcissistic abuse may engage in self-harming acts to cope with their mental distress. Self-harm gives momentary respite from misery, but it can have major long-term effects for physical and mental health.

Narcissistic abuse has catastrophic consequences for its victims, inflicting severe emotional, psychological, and occasionally bodily injury. Narcissistic abuse can cause long-term harm, ranging from poor self-esteem and anxiety to severe PTSD and autoimmune illnesses.

Victims must identify the impact of narcissistic abuse in their life and seek treatment and support to recover from their experiences. Therapy, support groups, and self-care routines can help victims recover their self-esteem, reclaim their sense of identity, and stop the pattern of abuse.

CHAPTER 5: CHILDHOOD COPING MECHANISMS AND RESPONSES TO ABUSE.

Children who grow up in abusive or narcissistic situations may develop coping strategies to adapt to their surroundings and protect themselves from further damage. These coping methods, while initially beneficial for survival, can have serious consequences for adult relationships and psychological growth.

Hyper-Vigilance

Hypervigilance is a frequent coping technique acquired as a response to maltreatment. Children raised in unstable or volatile situations tend to continually scan their surroundings for indicators of danger. This increased level of attention might help them anticipate and avoid possible hazards, but it can also cause persistent tension and worry.

- Relationship hypervigilance: Adults who were reared in abusive circumstances may find it difficult to trust others and build solid ties. They may be hypersensitive to minor indications or actions that indicate possible damage, making it difficult to build personal connections.

- Chronic hypervigilance can have a negative impact on mental health, resulting in symptoms such as anxiety, sleeplessness, and hyperarousal. Even in safe surroundings, people may struggle to relax or let down their guard.

Avoidance and Denial

Another popular coping strategy is avoidance and denial. Children who are unable to flee or confront their abusers may learn to detach from their feelings or pretend that the abuse isn't happening in order to cope with the anguish.

- Avoidance in Relationships: Adults who have developed avoidance coping methods may struggle to face confrontation or communicate their feelings in relationships. They may avoid uncomfortable talks or shut down emotionally in order to shield themselves from future trauma.

- Impact on Personal Development: Avoidance coping methods can stifle personal growth and development by preventing people from taking chances or following their dreams for fear of failure or rejection. This might cause emotions of stagnation and discontent in life.

People-Pleasing

Some youngsters raised in violent situations learn to adapt by becoming people pleasers. They learn to prioritize others' wants and aspirations over their own in order to avoid conflict and achieve favor.

- Codependent relationships: Adults who acquire people-pleasing coping techniques may find it difficult to articulate their own demands and limits. They may become immersed in codependent relationships, forsaking their own well-being for the sake of others.

  Constantly seeking external validation can have a negative impact on self-esteem since people may develop to rely on others' approval to feel worthwhile or lovable. When affirmation is not given, feelings of emptiness or inadequacy may arise.

Perfectionism

Perfectionism is another coping technique that may emerge in reaction to abuse. Children who are chastised or punished for their mistakes may develop a desire for perfection in order to avoid criticism and obtain praise.

- High expectations: Adults who adopt perfectionistic coping methods may establish impossible high expectations for themselves in order to escape criticism or rejection. They may associate their value with their accomplishments or performance, resulting in persistent stress and burnout.

- Impact on Relationships: Perfectionism may strain relationships because people struggle to accept flaws in themselves or others. They may become critical or judgmental of themselves and people around them, causing friction and dissatisfaction in relationships.

How Do These Mechanisms Impact Adult Relationships and Personal Development

Coping techniques learned in childhood in reaction to abuse can have a substantial impact on adult relationships and personal development.

- Impact on Intimate Relationships: Coping techniques like as hypervigilance, avoidance, people-pleasing, and perfectionism can all impede the capacity to have healthy, rewarding relationships. Individuals may struggle to trust others, communicate their feelings, or set boundaries, resulting in difficulty initiating and maintaining personal relationships.

- Repetition of Patterns: Without help, people may find themselves repeating the same patterns of behavior and relationships they learnt as children. They may unknowingly seek for partners who are similar to their abusive caretakers, or they may repeat past control and manipulative dynamics.

- Stagnation and dissatisfaction: Coping mechanisms learned in infancy might impede human growth and development. Individuals may become locked in behaviors of avoidance, denial, or perfectionism that impede them from achieving their objectives and living satisfying lives.

- Impact on Mental Health: Coping techniques can cause persistent stress and worry, which can be detrimental to one's mental health. Individuals may exhibit signs of despair, anxiety, or PTSD, as well as physical health issues including sleeplessness, chronic pain, and autoimmune illnesses.

Coping mechanisms formed throughout childhood in reaction to abuse can have long-term consequences for adult relationships and psychological development. Whether it's hypervigilance, avoidance, people-pleasing, or perfectionism, these coping techniques influence how people navigate the environment and connect with others.

Recognizing and comprehending these coping strategies is the first step toward recovery and progress. Individuals can learn to recognize and question maladaptive coping habits, create healthy ways of interacting to themselves and others, and eventually reclaim their life from the legacy of abuse

via treatment, self-reflection, and peer support.

CHAPTER SIX: PARENTIFICATION AND ROLE REVERSAL

Explanation of Parentification and its Impact

Parentification is a phenomena in which a kid is pushed to act as a parent or caretaker for their own parents or siblings. This can happen for a number of reasons, including parental neglect, substance addiction, mental illness, and divorce. When a kid is parentified, they are deprived of their own childhood and made to take on obligations and burdens that should be carried by adults. This can have long-term implications on the child's emotional and psychological development.

Types of Parentification

- In instrumental parentification, the kid assumes practical chores such as cooking, cleaning, and caring for younger siblings. They may become surrogate parents for their siblings, offering emotional support and direction in the absence of proper parental care.

- Emotional parentification happens when a kid is expected to meet their parent's emotional needs. They may act as their parent's confidant, therapist, or mediator, offering emotional support and validation in the absence of good adult connections.

Impact of Parentification

- Loss of Childhood: Parentification denies children the right to a carefree childhood. Instead of spending time with friends, enjoying hobbies, and exploring their interests, parentified youngsters are saddled with adult obligations and anxieties.

- Parentification throws a significant emotional weight on children, who are unprepared to deal with their parents' complicated emotions and conflicts. They may feel overwhelmed, nervous, and alone, unable to seek assistance or support for their own needs.

- Identity Confusion: Parentified children frequently struggle to form a strong sense of self and identity. They may define themselves primarily in terms of their caring responsibilities, lacking a strong feeling of autonomy and independence.

- Relationship Difficulties: Parentification can make it difficult to build and sustain good relationships. Children who have been parentified may fail to trust others, communicate their needs, or set boundaries, resulting in codependent or unhealthy relationships in maturity.

- Parentification is linked to a variety of mental health concerns, including sadness, anxiety, PTSD, and personality disorders. Children who have been parentified have a higher risk of chronic stress, low self-esteem, and emotional dysregulation.

Case Studies and Personal Stories

Case Study #1: Sarah

Sarah was raised in a family where her mother suffered from acute depression. Sarah was responsible for cooking, cleaning, and caring for her younger siblings since she was very little. She became her mother's confidant, listening to her problems and attempting to console her. Despite her best efforts, Sarah felt overwhelmed and unsupported, unable to seek assistance for her own emotional needs. As an adult, Sarah suffers from chronic anxiety and poor self-esteem, making it difficult to build and sustain good relationships.

Case Study #2: Michael

Michael's parents split when he was five years old, leaving him to look after his younger sister while his mother worked long hours to maintain the family. Michael took on the role of protector and provider, sheltering his sister from his parents' fight while also ensuring that they had food and a roof over their heads. Despite his best attempts, Michael felt lonely and isolated, aching for his missing parents' care and attention. As an adult, Michael has bitterness and animosity against his parents, as well as trouble trusting others and forging personal connections.

Personal Story: Maria.

Maria grew raised with an alcoholic father. Maria assumed responsibility for caring for her younger siblings, making meals, and cleaning the house from an early age, while her mother worked many jobs to support the family. Despite her efforts to keep the family together, Maria felt ignored and abandoned by her parents, who were preoccupied with their own drug issues. As an adult, Maria has emotions of worthlessness and inadequacy, as well as problems creating and sustaining meaningful relationships.

Parentification is a type of emotional abuse in which children are stripped of their childhood and forced to accept adult obligations and problems. Parentified children do not receive the care and attention they require to flourish, whether it is cooking meals, cleaning the house, or providing emotional support to their parents or siblings. Case studies and personal anecdotes demonstrate the tremendous and long-term influence of parentification on children's emotional and psychological well-being. It is critical for parents and caregivers to detect the indicators of parentification and take action to safeguard their children from this negative dynamic. By giving children the love, support, and stability they require to develop and flourish, we can help break the cycle of parentification and guarantee that every kid has the chance to have a happy and healthy childhood.

CHAPTER 7: DYNAMICS OF THE NARCISSISTIC FAMILY SYSTEM

Detailed Analysis of Family Roles

In a narcissistic family structure, each member is assigned a specific position that helps to preserve the family's dysfunctional dynamics. These roles are frequently inflexible and hierarchical, with the narcissistic parent wielding power and influence over the other family members. Understanding these roles is critical for detecting how narcissistic abuse spreads across the family structure.

The Narcissistic Parent

The narcissistic parent is at the heart of the narcissistic family structure, prioritizing his or her own needs and wishes over those of the rest of the family. The narcissistic parent craves approval and praise from others, and uses manipulation, compulsion, and emotional abuse to keep control over their children.

- Characteristics: The narcissistic parent exhibits grandiosity, entitlement, and a lack of empathy for others. They may appear charismatic and appealing in public, but behind closed doors, they are manipulative and domineering.

- The narcissistic parent maintains control over the family by intimidation, gaslighting, and emotional manipulation. They may require continual attention and affirmation from their children, using guilt, shame, or threats to retain control.

The Enabler

The enabler is usually a non-narcissistic parent or caregiver who condones the narcissistic parent's behavior and works with them to keep the dysfunctional family structure together. To protect the narcissistic parent, the enabler may choose to ignore the abuse or actively engage in gaslighting and manipulation.

- Characteristics: The facilitator is frequently meek and obedient, putting the narcissistic parent's wants ahead of their own or their children's. They may explain or rationalize the narcissistic parent's conduct, making explanations for it or downplaying the severity of the abuse.

- The enabler facilitates the narcissistic parent's conduct by justifying their acts and minimizing the consequences of their abuse on the family. They may also work with the narcissistic parent to blame or invalidate other family members who question their authority.

The Golden Child

The golden kid is the narcissistic parent's preferred child, who enjoys preferential care and advantages at the expense of their siblings. The golden kid is frequently trained to be a reflection of the narcissistic parent, embracing their ideals, beliefs, and behaviors.

- Characteristics: The narcissistic parent frequently showers the golden kid with praise, attention, and presents. They may be raised to feel that they are superior to their siblings and deserve special attention and privileges.

- The golden kid provides the narcissistic parent with recognition, adoration, and support. They might be utilized as a pawn in the narcissistic parent's manipulative methods, pitted against their siblings or other family members.

The Scapegoat

The scapegoat is a family member who is held accountable for the dysfunction and difficulties inside the family structure. They are frequently singled out for criticism, humiliation, and punishment by their narcissistic parent, who exploits them as a convenient scapegoat for their own flaws and insecurity.

- Characteristics: The scapegoat is usually a family member who questions the narcissistic parent's authority and control. They may be independent, loud, or nonconformist, refusing to participate in the narcissistic parent's manipulative games.

- The role of the scapegoat is to shift attention away from the narcissistic parent's own faults and shortcomings. They may face frequent criticism, gaslighting, and emotional abuse from their narcissistic parent and other family members.

The Lost Child

The lost kid is a family member who withdraws from the dysfunctional family structure, seeking peace and sanctuary in their own inner world. The lost kid may be disregarded or neglected by the narcissistic parent, who is too consumed with their own wants and desires to consider their child's welfare.

- Characteristics: The lost kid is usually timid, shy, and withdrawn, preferring to escape into fantasy or imagination rather to deal with the chaos and disorder in their familial setting.

- The lost kid acts as a mute witness of the instability within the family structure, seeking sanctuary from the chaos and strife by retreating into their own inner world. They may be disregarded or neglected by the narcissistic parent, who is too obsessed with their own demands and desires to consider their child's well-being.

How These Roles Continue the Cycle of Abuse.

Each position in the narcissistic family system contributes to the cycle of abuse and dysfunction within the family. By giving distinct responsibilities to each family member, the narcissistic parent maintains control and manipulation over their children, ensuring that their own wants and wishes take precedence over all others.

- Supporting conduct: The enabler collaborates with the narcissistic parent to keep the dysfunctional family structure going by supporting their conduct and minimizing the consequences of their abuse on the family. Enabling the narcissistic parent maintains the family's cycle of abuse and dysfunction.

- Golden Child Syndrome: The golden child is a source of narcissistic supply for the narcissistic parent, offering recognition, adoration, and support. By training the golden kid to be a mirror image of themselves, the narcissistic parent guarantees that their heritage of control and manipulation is passed down to future generations.

- Scapegoating Dynamics: The scapegoat is a handy target for the narcissistic parent's own weaknesses and anxieties, diverting focus away from their own flaws and deficiencies. By scapegoating the scapegoat, the narcissistic parent retains control and manipulation over the rest of the family, ensuring that their own demands and wishes take precedence over anything else.

- Lost kid Withdrawal: The lost kid retreats from the chaos of the family structure, seeking consolation and sanctuary in their own inner world. By retreating from the instability and conflict of their familial setting, the lost kid maintains the family's cycle of abuse and dysfunction, ensuring that their own needs and wishes are disregarded or forgotten.

The dynamics of a narcissistic family structure are defined by rigid roles and hierarchies, with the narcissistic parent exercising control and manipulation over their offspring. By assigning particular responsibilities to each family member, the narcissistic parent guarantees that their own wants and desires take precedence over all else, continuing the cycle of abuse and dysfunction in the family.

Recognizing these roles is critical to understanding how narcissistic abuse occurs within the family system and overcoming its harmful effect. Individuals may begin to recover from the scars of narcissistic abuse and reclaim their life from the dysfunctional legacy by seeking treatment, support, and self-awareness.

CHAPTER EIGHT: THE NARCISSISTIC ABUSE CYCLE

An in-depth look of the cycle: Idealization, Devaluation, Discard, and Hoovering

The narcissistic abuse cycle is a pattern of behavior that is regularly observed in interactions with narcissists. It is divided into four stages: idealization, devaluation, discard, and hoovering. Understanding each phase of the cycle is critical for recognizing and overcoming the harmful dynamics of narcissistic abuse.

Idealization

In the idealization phase, the narcissist lavishes their target with love, adoration, and attention, portraying themselves as the ideal lover or friend. They may utilize love bombing methods, such as lavish gifts, regular communication, and vows of adoration, to establish a strong relationship with their target.

- Love Bombing: The narcissist bombards their victim with romantic gestures, praises, and confessions of love, making them feel unique and wanted.

- Mirroring: The narcissist reflects their target's interests, values, and personality features, giving the impression of similarity and connection.

- Future Faking: The narcissist entices their target into the relationship by making extravagant promises about the future, such as marriage, children, and a luxurious lifestyle.

Devaluation

Once the narcissist has gained their target's affection and trust, they start devaluing and criticizing them, eroding their self-esteem and confidence. The devaluation phase is marked by manipulation, gaslighting, and emotional abuse as the narcissist attempts to exert power and dominance over their victim.

- Gaslighting occurs when the narcissist rejects, dismisses, or twists the truth of their target's experiences, leading them to question their own senses and recollections.

- Criticism and Blame: The narcissist criticizes and blames their victim for their own flaws and failings, transferring their anxieties onto them.

- Silent Treatment: The narcissist withholds affection and communication from their victim, leaving them confused, nervous, and yearning for affirmation.

Discard

During the discard phase, the narcissist abruptly terminates the connection or withdraws affection and attention from their victim, leaving them feeling abandoned, bewildered, and distraught. The discard phase may be triggered by perceived slights or threats to the narcissist's ego, as they want to maintain control and authority over their victim.

- Abandonment: A narcissist abandons their victim without warning or explanation, making them feel rejected and discarded.

- The narcissist may triangulate their target by introducing them to a new love partner or friend, manipulating and controlling them via envy and competitiveness.

- Idealization of New Supply: The narcissist presents their new love partner or acquaintance as the ideal substitute for their target, increasing their emotions of rejection and inadequacy.

Hoovering

After dismissing their victim, the narcissist may try to get them back into the relationship or friendship by using deception, guilt, and false promises to reclaim control and authority over them. The hoovering phase is distinguished by a cycle of push and pull, in which the narcissist swings between affection and harshness in order to keep their victim emotionally committed in the relationship.

- Hoovering Tactics: The narcissist may employ a variety of strategies to entice their victim back into the relationship, including apologies, promises of reform, and protestations of love.

- Intermittent Reinforcement: The narcissist alternates between warm gestures and frigid indifference, keeping their victim emotionally committed in the relationship by pushing and pulling.

- Manipulative Behavior: The narcissist utilizes guilt, shame, and manipulation to push their victim into returning to the relationship, taking advantage of their vulnerabilities and insecurities.

How to Identify and Break the Cycle

Recognizing and breaking out from the narcissistic abuse cycle necessitates awareness, self-reflection, and boundary establishing. Here are some strategies for recognizing and breaking the cycle of narcissistic abuse:

- Educate Yourself: Learn about the strategies and patterns of narcissistic abuse so you can identify them in your own relationships.

- Trust Your Instincts: Even if the narcissist uses gaslighting or manipulation to make you doubt yourself, trust your instincts and intuition.

- Set clear boundaries with the narcissist to protect yourself from further abuse and manipulation. Communicate your limits assertively and consistently, and impose penalties if they are crossed.

- Seek Support: For affirmation and encouragement, contact friends, family members, or support groups.

Surround yourself with supporters who can help you overcome the hurdles of breaking free from narcissistic abuse.

- Self-Care: Put your own well-being first by participating in activities that improve physical, emotional, and mental health. Take pauses when required, use relaxation techniques, and seek professional assistance if necessary.

- Detoxify Your Environment: Minimize or avoid interaction with the narcissist to reduce their capacity to influence and control you. Build a network of friends and family members who can offer emotional support and affirmation while you recover from narcissistic abuse.

- Seek Therapy: Consult a certified mental health expert who specializes in narcissistic abuse rehabilitation. Therapy may provide a safe and supportive environment in which to process your experiences, recover from trauma, and create healthy coping mechanisms for the future.

The narcissistic abuse cycle is a pattern of conduct that includes idealization, devaluation, rejection, and hoovering. Understanding each phase of the cycle is critical for recognizing and overcoming the harmful dynamics of narcissistic abuse. By educating yourself, setting boundaries, finding support, practicing self-care, and seeking treatment, you can escape the pattern of narcissistic abuse and reclaim your life from manipulation and control. Remember that recovering from narcissistic abuse is a process, but with patience and support, you will emerge stronger and more resilient than before.

CHAPTER 9: SELF-PERCEPTION IN THE MIDST OF ABUSE.

The Effects of Narcissistic Abuse on Self-Identity

Narcissistic abuse can have a significant and negative influence on a person's self-perception and identity. Narcissists' continuous manipulation, gaslighting, and emotional abuse may undermine one's self-esteem, leaving them confused, useless, and helpless. Understanding how narcissistic abuse impacts self-identity is critical for recovery and regaining one's sense of self.

Erosion of self-esteem

Narcissistic abuse frequently begins with idealization, in which the narcissist lavishes their target with love, attention, and adoration. However, this idealization is frequently fleeting, giving way to devaluation as the narcissist continues to criticise, insult, and undermine their target's self-worth. Over time, the relentless torrent of criticism and gaslighting may destroy the target's self-esteem, making them feel worthless, inadequate, and unlovable.

Identity Confusion

Narcissistic abuse can also cause identity confusion as the target tries to reconcile the narcissist's inconsistent signals and expectations for them. The narcissist may insist that their victim adhere to their idealized picture of them, suffocating their genuine self-expression and originality. As a result, the target may lose touch with their own wants, needs, and desires, leaving them feeling confused, empty, and disconnected from their own self.

Emotional Dependence

Another result of narcissistic abuse is emotional reliance, in which the target becomes progressively dependant on the narcissist for validation, acceptance, and self-worth. The narcissist employs manipulative techniques such as love bombing and intermittent reinforcement to keep their victim emotionally involved in the relationship, making it difficult for them to escape the cycle of abuse. As a result, the target may feel stuck and helpless, unable to express their autonomy or independence.

Tools to Separate Self-Worth from the Abuser's Manipulation

To break away from the hold of narcissistic abuse, one must first separate one's self-worth from the abuser's manipulation, and then recover a feeling of autonomy and power over one's life. While this process might be difficult, there are various tools and tactics that can assist people traverse the path to healing and self-reclamation.

Establishing Boundaries

Establishing and enforcing clear boundaries is one of the most critical strategies for separating one's self-worth from the manipulation of an abuser. limits are crucial for safeguarding oneself from additional abuse while also stating one's own needs, interests, and limits. Individuals may retake control and agency over their own life by talking directly with the narcissist and refusing to endure more abuse.

Cultivating self-compassion

Self-compassion is another effective strategy for divorcing one's value from the abuser's manipulation. Individuals who practice self-compassion can learn to treat themselves with love, understanding, and acceptance, even in the face of narcissistic criticism and abuse. Self-compassion is accepting one's own sorrow and suffering with warmth and empathy, as opposed to judgment and self-criticism.

Challenging Negative Beliefs

Narcissistic abuse frequently instills negative and self-limiting thoughts in the victim, such as "I am unworthy" or "I am unlovable." Challenging these negative thoughts and replacing them with more powerful and affirming beliefs is critical to developing self-esteem and self-worth. Cognitive-behavioral therapy (CBT) strategies like cognitive restructuring and thought challenging can help you recognize and challenge harmful ideas while replacing them with more positive and adaptive ones.

Creating a Support Network

Creating a support network of friends, family members, and mental health experts who can offer validation, support, and encouragement is critical for recovery from narcissistic abuse. Surrounding oneself with allies who understand and affirm one's experiences might make people feel less alone and lonely on their road to healing and self-reclamation. Individuals seeking support and affirmation as they traverse the hurdles of healing from narcissistic abuse may find value in support groups, internet forums, and therapy.

CHAPTER 10: REDISCOVERING YOURSELF

Steps to Reclaim Your Identity Following Abuse

Reclaiming one's identity after being abused, particularly narcissistic abuse, is a critical step toward healing and reconstructing a meaningful life. While the process of rediscovering oneself might be difficult, there are certain measures that people can take to recover their identity and establish their individuality.

1. Self-reflection and Awareness: Begin by practicing self-reflection and introspection to develop a better knowledge of yourself and your experiences. Take time to consider your values, beliefs, strengths, and limitations. Journaling, therapy, and meditation can be effective techniques for enhancing self-awareness and clarifying your identity and aspirations.

2. Determine your core values and priorities: Determine your primary beliefs and priorities, then use them as guiding principles throughout your life. Consider what is most important to you in terms of relationships, job, personal development, and well-being. Aligning your behaviors and decisions with your inner beliefs might help you live a more honest and fulfilled life that represents your true self.

3. Establish boundaries and prioritize self-care: Set clear boundaries with people to safeguard your physical, emotional, and psychological health. Learn to say no to things that deplete your energy or undermine your ideals, and instead emphasize self-care activities that nourish and refill you. Setting boundaries and prioritizing self-care are critical steps toward recovering your autonomy and asserting your needs and preferences.

4. Discover your passions and interests: Reconnect with the interests and hobbies that make you happy and fulfilled.

Make time for hobbies that inspire your enthusiasm and creativity, such as painting, writing, hiking, or dancing. Exploring your hobbies and interests might help you reconnect with your true self and find what makes you exceptional.

5. Develop Healthy Relationships: Surround yourself with loving and nurturing connections that will inspire and strengthen you. Seek for friends, relatives, and mentors who value and celebrate your authentic self, and avoid toxic or abusive people who damage your self-esteem. Building good connections is critical to regaining your confidence and self-esteem.

6. Address negative self-talk and limiting beliefs: Challenge negative self-talk and limiting ideas that are affecting your self-esteem and confidence. Replace self-critical ideas with more compassionate and uplifting comments, and use affirmations to emphasize your qualities and skills. CBT approaches can help identify and challenge negative thinking patterns.

7. Embrace growth and change: Accept development and change as normal parts of the human experience. Recognize your ability to change and grow beyond your previous experiences, and welcome new possibilities for learning and personal growth. Accepting development and change may help you go forward with confidence and resilience, knowing that you can make a better future for yourself.

Creating A New, Healthy Self-Image

Building a new, healthy self-image involves time, self-compassion, and a commitment to your own development and well-being. Here are some techniques for developing a good and empowered self-image:

1. Practice self-compassion: Self-compassion is treating yourself with care, understanding, and acceptance, especially during tough situations. Recognize your skills and successes, and forgive yourself for any apparent flaws or errors. Self-compassion is vital for developing a healthy, resilient self-image.

2. Celebrate Your Achievements: Celebrate your accomplishments, no matter how minor or inconsequential they may appear. Recognize your development and growth, and be proud of your achievements. Celebrating your accomplishments may increase your self-esteem and strengthen your faith in your talents and value.

3. Surround yourself with positivity: Surround yourself with optimism by seeking out uplifting and inspirational people in your life. Surround yourself with people who support and encourage you, and consume media and information that promotes optimism and empowerment.

Surrounding oneself with positivity can help you overcome negative self-perceptions and increase your self-confidence.

4. Practice self-care: Prioritize self-care activities that will nourish your body, mind, and soul. Exercise, meditation, and spending time in nature are all good ways to relax, relieve stress, and improve general well-being. Prioritizing self-care is critical for maintaining a positive self-image and fostering a feeling of inner harmony and balance.

5. Seek Professional Help as Needed: If you are fighting to rebuild your self-image or overcome unfavorable self-perceptions, don't be afraid to seek professional help from a therapist or counselor. A skilled mental health professional may offer advice, support, and strategies for overcoming low self-esteem and developing a positive self-image.

Reclaiming your identity and developing a healthy self-image after trauma is a path that needs bravery, introspection, and endurance. By taking proactive measures to reconnect with yourself, create boundaries, prioritize self-care, and confront negative self-perceptions, you may start to recover your self-esteem and express your independence. Remember that healing is a gradual process, so be patient and kind to yourself as you begin on this path of self-discovery and self-reclamation. With effort and persistence, you may develop a positive and empowered self-image that represents your genuine value and potential.

CHAPTER 11: EFFECTIVE COPING STRATEGIES.

Practical Tips for the Gray Rock Method and Other Techniques

When dealing with narcissistic abuse, having good coping mechanisms is critical for sustaining emotional well-being and protecting oneself from future harm. In this chapter, we'll look at practical guidance on the Gray Rock Method and other ways for dealing with narcissists.

The Gray Rock Method

The Gray Rock Method is a strategy for reducing encounters with narcissists and limiting their potential to influence and dominate you. The Gray Rock Method's primary principle is to become as dull and unresponsive as possible, lowering the narcissist's interest in you and desire to interact with you.

How to implement the Gray Rock Method:

- Limit Emotional Expression: Avoid expressing any strong emotions, happy or negative, in the company of the narcissist. Keep a neutral and controlled demeanor at all times.

- Provide Bland comments: When communicating with a narcissist, make your comments brief, basic, and free of emotional substance. Stick to facts and avoid providing personal information or opinions.

- Avoid Confrontation: Avoid arguing or confronting the narcissist, since this will just fuel their desire for drama and attention. Disengage from the conversation and, if feasible, leave the situation.

- Set Firm limits: Communicate clear limits with the narcissist and continually enforce them. Be aggressive in communicating your boundaries, and refuse to allow any infractions.

- Prioritize self-care activities that will improve your physical, emotional, and psychological well-being. Engage in things that make you happy and relax, and seek help from friends, family, or a therapist if necessary.

Other Coping Techniques

In addition to the Gray Rock Method, there are numerous more coping strategies that can assist you negotiate relationships with narcissists while protecting your mental and emotional health.

1. Consider practicing the No interaction Rule, which is avoiding all communication and interaction with the narcissist whenever feasible. This might help you get away from their harmful influence and concentrate on your own healing and rehabilitation.

2. Practice Emotional distance: Reframe your thoughts and views about the relationship to help you create emotional

distance from the narcissist. Remember that their conduct reflects their own troubles and fears, not your worth or value as a person.

3. Create a Support Network: Surround yourself with sympathetic and understanding people who can offer affirmation, encouragement, and practical help as you negotiate the difficulties of coping with narcissistic abuse. Joining a support group or online forum for victims of narcissistic abuse might also assist.

4. Practice Self-Reflection: Take time to consider your own ideas, feelings, and behaviors in regard to the narcissistic relationship. Investigate any patterns or dynamics that may have led to the abusive dynamic, and focus on creating healthy coping methods and boundaries in the future.

5. Seek practitioner Help: Seek therapy or counseling from a certified mental health practitioner who specializes in narcissistic abuse rehabilitation. Therapy may provide a

secure and supportive environment in which to process your experiences, recover from trauma, and build effective coping mechanisms for dealing with narcissists.

Real-world Applications and Success Stories

To demonstrate the usefulness of coping methods such as the Gray Rock Method and other tactics, consider some real-life examples and success stories from people who have used these strategies in their own lives.

Case Study #1: Sarah

Sarah had been in a toxic relationship with her narcissistic spouse for many years. After learning about the Gray Rock Method, she began using it everytime she interacted with her spouse. Sarah was able to lessen the intensity of their disagreements while also protecting her own emotional well-being by keeping emotional distance and responding blandly. Sarah eventually decided to end the relationship and enforce strict No Contact, allowing her to focus on her own rehabilitation and recovery.

Case Study #2: Michael

Michael grew up with a narcissistic dad who frequently ridiculed and belittled him, causing him to lose self-esteem and confidence. Michael was able to lessen the impact of his parents' abuse on his mental and emotional health after learning about the Gray Rock Method and setting firm boundaries with them. With the help of a therapist and a supporting network of friends, Michael was able to restore his sense of self-worth and develop a stronger relationship with his mom based on mutual respect and limits.

Success Story: Maria.

Maria had been in a manipulative and controlling connection with a narcissist for several years. Maria was able to emotionally disengage from the toxic dynamic by using the Gray Rock Method and other coping mechanisms. By setting boundaries and emphasizing self-care, Maria was able to quit the connection and go on to other relationships that nourished and supported her.

Effective coping mechanisms, such as the Gray Rock Method and other tactics, are critical for dealing with narcissists and maintaining your mental and emotional health. Implementing these tactics, setting strong boundaries, and prioritizing self-care will allow you to restore your feeling of self-worth and autonomy in the face of narcissistic abuse. Remember that healing is a process, and it's OK to seek help from friends, family, or a therapist while you go through the difficulties of recovering from narcissistic abuse. With patience and determination, you can break away from narcissistic manipulation and live a better, healthier life for yourself.

CHAPTER 12: THE PATH OF HEALING

Establishing Healthy Boundaries With Abusers and Others

Setting appropriate boundaries is critical for safeguarding your mental, emotional, and physical well-being, particularly when dealing with abusers such as narcissists. We'll talk about how to set and keep boundaries with abusers and others in your life.

1. Establish Your Personal Boundaries: Determine what actions you consider acceptable and inappropriate. Consider what you are prepared to endure and what is unacceptable treatment from others.

2. Communicate Clearly: Establish aggressive and clear limits with the abuser or person. Use "I" statements to describe your wants and limitations, and communicate firmly and directly.

3. Enforce Consequences: Be ready to take action if your limits are broken. This might involve restricting contact with the abuser, leaving the relationship, or seeking help from authorities if required.

4. Surround yourself with supportive people who respect and acknowledge your boundaries. Seek out friends, family members, or support groups who can offer encouragement and help as you work to establish boundaries with abusers and others.

Strategies to Silence the Critical Inner Voice

The critical inner voice, which is frequently driven by toxic words from narcissists, can be a substantial impediment to healing. Here are some ways to silence the critical inner voice and cultivate self-compassion:

1. Develop Self-Awareness: Identify negative ideas and beliefs caused by your critical inner voice. Recognize when

these thoughts appear and counter them with more realistic and compassionate viewpoints.

2. Practice Self-Compassion: Be nice and compassionate to oneself, especially when dealing with negative thoughts. Remind yourself that it's alright to make mistakes and that you deserve love and acceptance exactly the way you are.

3. Challenge Negative thoughts: Confront your critical inner voice and challenge its negative thoughts. Replace them with more powerful and encouraging ideas about your own worth and value as a person.

4. Practice Gratitude: Practicing gratitude can reduce negative self-talk and promote a good outlook. Take time every day to think on what you're grateful for and admire about yourself.

Let Go of False Hope for Change in the Abuser

One of the most difficult components of recovering from narcissistic abuse is letting go of unrealistic expectations of the abuser's change. Here's how to go through this process:

1. Accept Reality: Despite your best efforts, it's doubtful that the abuser will modify their conduct. Recognize that their conduct reflects their own problems and fears, not your worth or value as a person.

2. Set fair Expectations: Recognize the abuser's limits and establish fair expectations for the relationship. Be honest with yourself about the probability of change, and prioritize self-care over attempting to change the abuser.

3. Prioritize Your Healing: Rather of trying to change the abuser, focus on your own healing and rehabilitation. Invest your time and energy in activities and relationships that promote your well-being.

4. Seek Support: Look for acceptance and encouragement from friends, family, or a therapist as you let go of false hope for change in the abuser. Surround yourself with allies who understand and support your decision to prioritize your own health.

Embracing self-compassion and resilience on the journey to recovery.

Accepting self-compassion and resilience is critical for navigating the path to recovery from narcissistic abuse. Here's how to develop these qualities:

1. Prioritize self-care activities like exercise, meditation, and nature time. Take pauses as required and heed to your body's signals for rest and relaxation.

2. Foster Resilience: Develop healthy coping processes and methods to manage stress and hardship. Concentrate on your strengths and achievements, and remind yourself of your capacity to overcome obstacles and disappointments.

3. Foster Connections: Build relationships with helpful persons that elevate and encourage you. Surround yourself with friends, family members, and mentors who understand and validate your experiences and can offer encouragement and support while you go through the obstacles of recovery.

4. Practice Forgiveness: Forgive yourself and the abuser as part of the healing process. Let go of your bitterness and anger against the abuser, and instead focus on relieving yourself of the emotional load of having those bad feelings.

The pathway to recovery from narcissistic abuse involves bravery, self-awareness, and perseverance. Setting appropriate boundaries with abusers and others, silencing the critical inner voice, letting go of mistaken hope for change in the abuser, and embracing self-compassion and resilience will help you restore your feeling of self-worth and autonomy. Remember that healing is a slow process, and it is OK to seek help from friends, family, or a therapist while you face the hurdles of rehabilitation. With effort and determination, you can overcome narcissistic abuse and create a better, healthier life for yourself.